List Of Songs

D1541134

TEARS IN HEAVEN

Words and Music by ERIC CLAPTON and WILL JENNINGS

DANCING QUEEN

YOUR SONG

Words and Music by ELTON JOHN and BERNIE TAUPIN

YESTERDAY

Words and Music by JOHN LENNON and PAUL McCARTNEY

UNCHAINED MELODY

Lyric by HY ZARET, Music by ALEX NORTH

WE ARE THE CHAMPIONS

LOVE ME TENDER

Words and Music by ELVIS PRESLEY and VERA MATSON

WE ARE THE WORLD

Words and Music by LIONEL RICHIE and MICHAEL JACKSON

IMAGINE

Words and Music by JOHN LENNON

CANDLE IN THE WIND

Words and Music by ELTON JOHN and BERNIE TAUPIN

FIELDS OF GOLD

Music and Lyrics by STING

YOU RAISE ME UP

Words and Music by BRENDAN GRAHAM and ROLF LOVLAND

FROM A DISTANCE

Words and Music by JULIE GOLD

ALL YOU NEED IS LOVE

Words and Music by JOHN LENNON and PAUL McCARTNEY

PENNY LANE

Words and Music by JOHN LENNON and PAUL McCARTNEY

HEY JUDE

Words and Music by JOHN LENNON and PAUL McCARTNEY

HERE COMES THE SUN

Words and Music by GEORGE HARRISON

EYE OF THE TIGER

Words and Music by FRANK SULLIVAN and JIM PETERIK

I WILL ALWAYS LOVE YOU

Words and Music by DOLLY PARTON

HAPPY

Words and Music by PHARRELL WILLIAMS

WHERE DO I BEGIN

Words by CARL SIGMAN, Music by FRANCIS LAI

(THEY LONG TO BE) CLOSE TO YOU

Lyrics by HAL DAVID, Music by BURT BACHARACH

CALIFORNIA DREAMIN'

Words and Music by JOHN PHILLIPS and MICHELLE PHILLIPS

RAINDROPS KEEP FALLIN' ON MY HEAD

Lyrics by HAL DAVID, Music by BURT BACHARACH

ROLLING IN THE DEEP

Words and Music by ADELE ADKINS and PAUL EPWORTH

A THOUSAND YEARS

Words and Music by ERIC CLAPTON and WILL JENNINGS

CHASING CARS

Words and Music by GARY LIGHTBODY, TOM SIMPSON, PAUL WILSON,
JONATHAN QUINN and NATHAN CONNOLLY

PIANO MAN

Words and Music by BILLY JOEL

A WHITER SHADE OF PALE

Words and Music by KEITH REID, GARY BROOKER and MATTHEW FISHER

THE LION SLEEPS TONIGHT

New Lyrics and Revised Music by GEORGE DAVID WEISS, HUGO PERETTI and LUIGI CREATORE

NIGHTS IN WHITE SATIN

Words and Music by JUSTIN HAYWARD

SMOKE ON THE WATER

Words and Music by RITCHIE BLACKMORE, IAN GILLAN, ROGER GLOVER,
JON LORD and IAN PAICE

QUE SERA, SERA
(WHATEVER WILL BE, WILL BE)

Words and Music by JAY LIVINGSTON and RAYMOND B. EVANS

TILL THERE WAS YOU

By MEREDITH WILLSON

BEAT IT

Words and Music by MICHAEL JACKSON

STAIRWAY TO HEAVEN

Words and Music by JIMMY PAGE and ROBERT PLANT

HOTEL CALIFORNIA

Words and Music by DON HENLEY, GLENN FREY and DON FELDER

TIME TO SAY GOODBYE

Words by LUCIO QUARANTOTTO and FRANK PETERSON, Music by FRANCESCO SARTORI

HIGHLAND CATHEDRAL

By MICHAEL KORB and ULRICH ROEVER

BELIEVER

Words and Music by DAN REYNOLDS, WAYNE SERMON, BEN McKEE, DANIEL
PLATZMAN, JUSTIN TRANTOR, MATTIAS LARSSON and ROBIN FREDRICKSSON

OPEN ARMS

Words and Music by STEVE PERRY and JONATHAN CAIN

SMOOTH

Words by ROB THOMAS, Music by ROB THOMAS and ITALL SHUR

THE RAINBOW CONNECTION

Words and Music by PAUL WILLIAMS and KENNETH L. ASCHER

JAILHOUSE ROCK

Words and Music by JERRY LEIBER and MIKE STOLLER

WONDERFUL TONIGHT

Words and Music by ERIC CLAPTON

EVERY BREATH YOU TAKE

Music and Lyrics by STING

WITH A LITTLE HELP FROM MY FRIENDS

Words and Music by JOHN LENNON and PAUL McCARTNEY

HAPPY TOGETHER

Words and Music by GARRY BONNER and ALAN GORDON

THOSE WERE THE DAYS

Words and Music by GENE RASKIN

WE'VE ONLY JUST BEGUN

Words and Music by ROGER NICHOLS and PAUL WILLIAMS

ALFIE

Words by HAL DAVID Music by BURT BACHARACH

TOP OF THE WORLD

Words and Music by JOHN BETTIS and RICHARD CARPENTER

HOW DEEP IS YOUR LOVE

Words and Music by BARRY GIBB, ROBIN GIBB and MAURICE GIBB

CANDLE IN THE WIND 1997

Words and Music by ELTON JOHN and BERNIE TAUPIN

25 OR 6 TO 4

Words and Music by ROBERT LAMM

CAN'T TAKE MY EYES OFF OF YOU

Words and Music by BOB CREWE and BOB GAUDIO

TIME AFTER TIME

Words and Music by CYNDI LAUPER and ROB HYMAN

THE LONG AND WINDING ROAD

Words and Music by JOHN LENNON and PAUL McCARTNEY

YOU DON'T KNOW WHAT LOVE IS

Words and Music by DON RAYE and GENE DePAUL

ALL OF ME

Words and Music by JOHN STEPHENS and TOBY GAD

D.S. al Coda

THE POWER OF LOVE

Words by MARY SUSAN APPLEGATE and JENNIFER RUSH Music by
CANDY DEROUGE and GUNTHER MENDE

D.S. al Fine

VIVA LA VIDA

Words and Music by GUY BERRYMAN, JON BUCKLAND, WILL CHAMPION and CHRIS MARTIN

THE FIRST TIME EVER I SAW YOUR FACE

Words and Music by EWAN MacCOLL

I'M A BELIEVER

Words and Music by NEIL DIAMOND

SPACE ODDITY

Words and Music by DAVID BOWIE

BOHEMIAN RHAPSODY

Words and Music by FREDDIE MERCURY

Shuffle feel, swing

Tempo I

74

HEAL THE WORLD

Words and Music by MICHAEL JACKSON

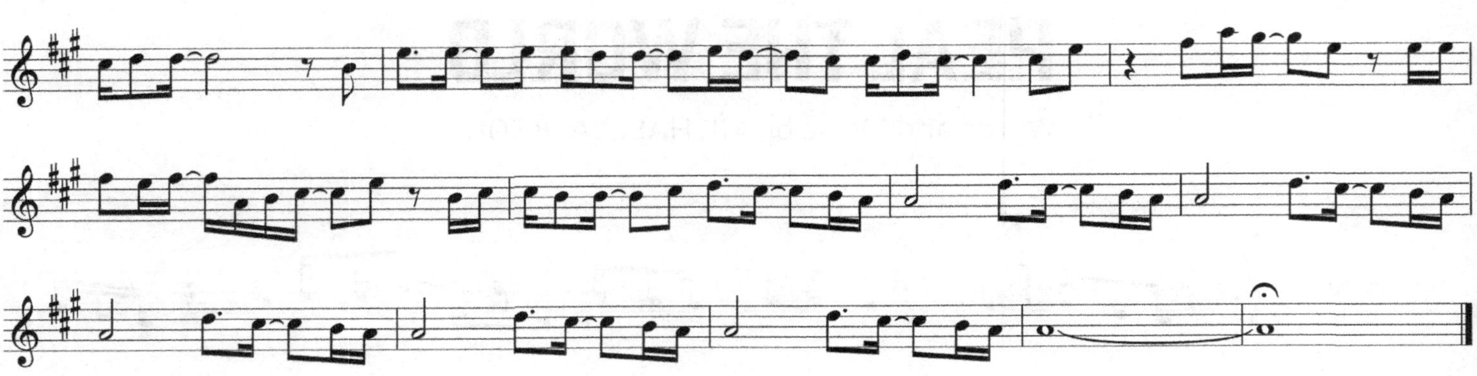

VIENNA

Words and Music by BILLY JOEL

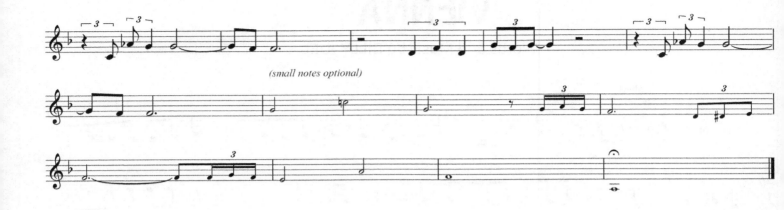

(small notes optional)

ANOTHER BRICK IN THE WALL

Words and Music by ROGER WATERS

LULLABYE (GOODNIGHT, MY ANGEL)

Words and Music by BILLY JOEL

Made in the USA
Monee, IL
15 December 2023

49413054R00046